Sparking the Invisible Drive

Decoding Motivation Theory for the Modern Mind

Freudian Trips

Copyright Page

Disclaimer

The views and opinions expressed in this book are those of the author(s) and do not necessarily reflect the official policy or position of any other agency, organization, employer, or company. The contents of this book are for informational and educational purposes only and are not intended to serve as professional advice, diagnosis, or treatment.

The information provided in this book is believed to be accurate and reliable as of the date of publication. However, it may include some errors or inaccuracies, and no warranty or guarantee is provided regarding the accuracy, timeliness, or applicability of the content.

Readers are encouraged to consult with professional philosophers, educators, or other qualified professionals where appropriate for personalized advice. The author(s) and publisher shall not be liable for any loss, damage, or harm caused or alleged to be caused, directly or indirectly, by the information or ideas contained, suggested, or referenced in this book.

By reading this book, the reader acknowledges and agrees that they are solely responsible for how they interpret and apply the information contained herein.

This book may also include references to other works, studies, and sources. These references are provided for further reading and exploration and do not imply endorsement or validation of the specific theories, viewpoints, or interpretations presented in those works.

Chapter 1: The Invisible Drive

Imagine you're at the bottom of a hill with a bicycle. Now, what pushes you to hop on and pedal up, feeling the wind against your face and sweat forming on your brow? It's not just about reaching the top. It's about the drive, the push, the spark inside you. That, dear reader, is motivation.

A. What is Motivation Anyway?

Motivation isn't just a word thrown around by life coaches on TV or something scribbled in bold letters on inspirational posters. At its core, motivation is the 'why' behind our actions. It's the emotional, psychological, and sometimes even physical nudge that says, "Hey, let's do this!" Think of it as the fuel for our life's engine.

But why the fuss about a term? Because motivation is more than a word; it's a theory that scientists, thinkers, and even business leaders have dissected for decades. In essence, Motivation Theory is our attempt to understand this drive, to make sense of why we do what we do.

B. Navigating the Modern World: Why Motivation Matters

Let's rewind a bit. Back in the day, survival was our primary motivation. Hunger? Hunt. Cold? Find shelter. But fast forward to today, our world isn't just about basic survival. It's packed with choices and possibilities.

Want to learn the piano? There's an app for that. Dream of starting a business? Resources are just a click away. Crave human connection? Dive into social media. With a world bursting with opportunities, understanding what truly motivates us becomes even more essential.

Imagine a scenario where you wake up, scroll through social media, and see a friend hiking a mountain. Another is starting a business, and yet another just baked the most mouth-watering cookies. Suddenly, the comfort of your bed doesn't seem so appealing. You want to do something too! But what? And more importantly, why?

That's where understanding motivation comes into play. It helps us navigate the choices, prioritize our desires, and ultimately, lead a life aligned with our true aspirations, rather than getting lost in the hustle and bustle.

C. A Sneak Peek into Our Journey

You might be thinking, "Okay, this is all great, but what am I diving into?" To quench your curiosity, here's a quick roadmap:

We'll explore the ancient thinkers who pondered motivation and the modern-day scientists who studied it like detectives on a mission.

We'll dive deep into the modern world's challenges, like technology's role in shaping our desires and how globalization has changed the motivation game.

Personal life, professional life, dark sides, and bright futures – we will discuss how motivation plays its part everywhere.

And finally, because we believe in equipping you with practical tools, we've got a toolkit waiting. This will help you not just understand motivation but harness it.

So, buckle up! Whether you're here out of sheer curiosity, a burning desire to understand yourself and others, or just because you liked the cover (wink!), we promise this journey through motivation will be enlightening, entertaining, and most importantly, empowering.

Note to readers: As we dive deeper into this topic, remember that motivation isn't a one-size-fits-all concept. Your 'why' is uniquely yours. Embrace it, understand it, and let it guide you. Happy reading!

Chapter 2: Tracing the Threads of Desire

Have you ever thought about the timeless allure of stories? Why does the tale of a determined hero, overcoming odds, or a person chasing a dream, resonate so deeply across ages? It's because at the heart of all stories is motivation - the age-old question of "Why?" Let's embark on a historical voyage to uncover the origins of understanding this drive.

A. Whispers from the Ancients: Philosophical Perspectives

Long before your favorite influencers talked about "hustle" and "grind", there were thinkers – we often call them philosophers – who sat under trees or in grand halls, pondering the essence of human drive.

1. Ancient Greece: A Thinker's Paradise

In Ancient Greece, the renowned philosopher Aristotle introduced a concept called 'telos'. No, it's not a mysterious spell from a fantasy novel! Telos simply means 'purpose' or 'end goal'. He believed that everything in nature, including humans, had a purpose. For humans, our purpose (or motivation) was to attain 'eudaimonia', a fancy term for happiness or flourishing. Simply put, Aristotle was onto something big: he realized that we humans are always chasing happiness.

2. The Eastern Enlightenment

Parallelly, in the East, philosophies like Buddhism and Confucianism shed light on human desires and motivations. Buddha spoke of the "Four Noble Truths" which revolved around understanding and managing desire to attain enlightenment. Similarly, Confucius believed in the principle of 'ren' or benevolence, which emphasized the importance of social harmony and personal virtue as motivational forces.

B. Diving into the Human Mind: Early Psychological Studies

Fast forward a few centuries, and we land in the age of the emerging science of the mind – psychology!

1. The Puzzle of Behavior

In the late 19th and early 20th century, scientists started observing behaviors - not just of humans but animals too. Ever heard of the story of Pavlov's dog salivating at the sound of a bell? This was an early experiment in understanding conditioned behaviors, highlighting how external factors can motivate actions.

2. The Freudian Slip into Motivation

No historical journey into psychology is complete without mentioning Sigmund Freud. He introduced the idea that our behaviors, our motivations, are driven by a mix of conscious and unconscious desires. So, if you've ever wondered why you suddenly craved chocolate or felt an urge to dance in the rain, Freud would probably say, "Ah, let's talk about your unconscious desires."

C. Structuring the Spark: The Birth of Formal Motivation Theory

While musings and experiments are fascinating, there came a time when thinkers decided to frame motivation into formal theories.

1. The Needs Pyramid

Ever feel like once you've achieved something, there's still something more you crave? Abraham Maslow had a similar idea. He visualized our motivations as a pyramid. At the base are our most basic needs, like food and safety. As you move up, there are needs like love, esteem, and right at the top, self-actualization - the desire to become the best version of oneself.

2. Beyond Rewards and Punishments

While many early theories revolved around the concept of rewards and punishments as the primary drivers of behavior, thinkers began to understand there was more to motivation. Concepts like intrinsic motivation – doing something because it feels good or right, rather than for a reward – started gaining ground.

Note to readers: Isn't it fascinating to realize that centuries ago, humans, just like us, pondered the same questions of purpose, drive, and desire? While our surroundings, technologies, and lifestyles have dramatically shifted, our quest to understand "why we do what we do" remains a timeless journey. As we delve deeper into the nuances of modern motivation theories, remember that this quest, this journey, is part of our shared human heritage.

Chapter 3: Meeting the Motivation Maestros

Imagine walking into a grand hall filled with the most brilliant minds, each one having a unique perspective on why we, as humans, act the way we do. In this chapter, let's shake hands (virtually, of course) with some of these trailblazers and get a glimpse of their groundbreaking ideas on motivation.

A. Climbing Maslow's Pyramid: The Hierarchy of Needs

Let's begin with a pyramid, but not the ones from Egypt. This pyramid was conceptualized by a man named Abraham Maslow.

1. The Base Layers: Picture a pyramid in your mind. At its wide base, Maslow placed our most fundamental needs - the essentials like food, water, and safety. Without these, we wouldn't get very far.

2. The Middle Magic: As we move up the pyramid, our needs become more social and emotional. Think friendship, family, and a sense of belonging. Above this is our desire for respect, self-esteem, and recognition.

3. The Pinnacle of Potential: At the very top sits a golden concept - self-actualization. This is the dreamy stage where we seek to achieve our full potential and pursue inner growth and creativity.

B. Herzberg's Illuminating Insights: The Two-Factor Theory

Next, meet Frederick Herzberg, who saw motivation as a two-sided coin.

1. The Hygiene Factors: These are the basics. They don't necessarily motivate us, but their absence can demotivate. Think of a comfortable office chair. It might not inspire you to work harder, but a wobbly one could definitely annoy you!

2. The Motivators: These are the real stars, the factors that truly drive us. Think achievement, responsibility, and growth. When these are present, we feel genuinely inspired and driven.

C. McClelland's Human Desires: The Theory of Needs

David McClelland took a slightly different route. Instead of pyramids or two-sided coins, he talked about three core needs.

1. Need for Achievement: Some of us have a burning desire to accomplish tasks, solve problems, or come out on top.

2. Need for Affiliation: This is all about relationships. People with a high need for affiliation crave friendly interactions and being part of a group.

3. Need for Power: No, it's not always about being a supervillain! This need revolves around influencing others and making an impact.

D. Lighting the Inner Flame: Deci and Ryan's Self-Determination Theory

Lastly, let's chat about Edward Deci and Richard Ryan. They delved deep into what makes activities personally meaningful.

1. Autonomy: We all love a bit of freedom, right? Autonomy is the desire to be the captain of our ship, to have choices and act in harmony with our self.

2. Competence: It's that wonderful feeling of "I've got this!" It's about mastering a skill or task.

3. Relatedness: Remember the joy of sharing a secret with a friend? That's relatedness – our desire to connect with others and feel a sense of belonging.

Note to readers: If you ever feel overwhelmed by what drives you, remember, you're not alone! Through history, great minds have pondered the same question. But more than the theories, it's crucial to reflect on what resonates with you. After all, you are the ultimate expert on your motivation. Let these theories be guiding stars, but always trust the compass of your heart.

Chapter 4: The Modern Motive Matrix

Picture this: You're surrounded by devices that ping, screens that glow, and a world that's increasingly blurred between the virtual and real. Ever stopped to ponder how this whirlwind of a world affects your drive? Welcome to the realm of motivation in our digital age.

A. Charting New Terrains: Motivation Theory's Modern Evolution

The 21st century hasn't just transformed our skylines and gadgets. It's also reshaped our understanding of motivation.

1. Beyond Basics: Gone are the days when motivations were seen as merely individual drives. Today, they're intertwined with collective consciousness, social dynamics, and even global movements. Our desires are not just about 'me' but also about 'we'.

2. Flexibility over Fixed: Earlier, theorists tried to put motivations into neat boxes (or pyramids!). But now, we realize motivations are fluid, changing with life stages, experiences, and even daily moods.

B. From Cables to Clouds: How Technology and Globalization Reframe our Drives

With screens in our pockets and the world at our fingertips, the global village isn't just a phrase—it's a reality.

1. A World without Walls: Thanks to globalization, we're not just competing or collaborating with our neighbors but with someone half a world away. This global perspective has amplified our need for self-improvement and continuous learning.

2. Instant Gratifications: Remember when you had to wait weeks for a letter? Now, it's all about instant messages, fast deliveries, and real-time updates. This craving for immediacy has reshaped our patience levels and how we view rewards.

C. Likes, Shares, and the Drive to Shine: Social Media's Role in Motivation

Ah, the double-edged sword of the digital age: Social Media. It's changed not just how we communicate but also why we act the way we do.

1. The Showcase Culture: Each time we post, it's like stepping onto a stage. We're driven by the desire for validation, feedback, and the dopamine rush of notifications.

2. Comparison Lanes: With every scroll, we're not just consuming content. We're often comparing—lifestyles, achievements, even happiness levels. This comparison game has a profound impact on our motivations, sometimes pushing us to aspire, but other times, plunging us into self-doubt.

3. Virtual Communities: On the brighter side, social media has also allowed us to find our tribes, groups that share our passions, values, or dreams. These communities can be massive motivational boosters, fueling our drives and aspirations.

Note to readers: As we journey through the digital age, remember to occasionally pause and reflect. Understand what truly drives you. Is it your authentic self or the pressures of the pixelated screens? In this interconnected world, while it's vital to stay plugged in, it's equally crucial to sometimes unplug and tune into your inner motivations.

Chapter 5: Your Inner Engine: The Power of Personal Motivation

Picture yourself as a boat. Sometimes, the winds are in your favor, pushing you forward effortlessly. At other times, the seas are calm, and it's up to you to row. That force you use to row, even when things seem tough, that's personal motivation. Dive in as we explore the magic and mechanics of this inner drive.

A. Personal Motivation: Why it's More than Just a Buzzword

1. Your Personal Fuel: Just as cars need fuel and plants need sunlight, we humans need motivation. It's the energy that gets us out of bed, drives our decisions, and shapes our dreams.

2. Navigating Life's Waves: Life isn't always smooth sailing. There are highs and lows, storms and calms. Personal motivation is the compass and anchor that helps us navigate these varied seas.

B. Personal Growth: The Lush Garden of Motivation

Have you ever seen a plant twist and turn to face the sunlight? That's a lot like personal motivation guiding our growth.

1. Breaking the Shell: Just as seeds need to break their shell to grow into mighty trees, we too need motivation to push past our comfort zones and truly flourish.

2. Crafting the Best Version of You: It's easy to float through life, but to shape a meaningful and fulfilling journey requires motivation. Whether it's picking up a new skill, nurturing relationships, or overcoming fears, motivation plays a central role.

C. Turbocharging Your Drive: Strategies to Boost Personal Motivation

Feeling your inner engine slowing down? Here are some strategies to rev it up!

1. Vision Boards: Visualizing goals can be powerful. Create a board or a journal filled with images, quotes, and reminders of what you're aiming for. Let it be a daily source of inspiration.

2. Small Steps, Big Leaps: Instead of overwhelming yourself with a huge task, break it into bite-sized chunks. Celebrate each small victory—it's like a shot of motivational adrenaline!

3. Surround Yourself with Positivity: Be it uplifting music, motivational books, or encouraging friends, make sure your environment is a garden where motivation can bloom.

4. Reflect and Reconnect: Set aside quiet moments to reconnect with your 'why'. Reflect on what drove you in the past, what drives you now, and how that might change in the future.

5. Embrace Failures as Lessons: Remember, every setback is a setup for a comeback. Instead of getting demotivated by failures, view them as valuable lessons, steering you towards success.

Note to readers: Your journey is unique, dotted with dreams, challenges, joys, and lessons. At its core, driving this journey, is your personal motivation. Nurture it, cherish it, and let it light your path. As you turn each page of life, may your motivation shine bright, guiding you towards the stories you're destined to write.

Chapter 6: Fueling the Work Wheel: Motivation in the Office and Beyond

Ever wonder what makes Jane from accounting consistently deliver exceptional results? Or why Mike in marketing always seems pumped about his projects? Chances are, it's not just caffeine. It's the vibrant energy of motivation pulsing through the professional landscape. Let's navigate this bustling city of workplace motivation together.

A. Leaders, Captains, and the Motivational Beacon

When you think of a ship navigating the vast seas, it's the captain that charts the course. Similarly, in the professional realm, leaders and managers play a pivotal role in guiding motivation.

1. The Leader as a Mirror: Employees often look up to their leaders, drawing inspiration. If a leader is passionate and driven, it's like sunshine radiating throughout the team.

2. Building a Motivated Culture: It's not just about personal drive; leaders also shape the culture. A workplace that celebrates innovation, encourages risk-taking, and values feedback is like fertile soil where motivation sprouts effortlessly.

B. The Heartbeat of an Organization: Employee Engagement

1. More than Just a Job: When employees see their roles as more than just tasks, when they connect with the 'why' behind their 'what', that's when magic happens. Engaged employees don't just work; they bring visions to life.

2. Recognition and Rewards: Imagine working hard on a project and then... silence. Feels a bit empty, right? Recognizing efforts and celebrating achievements is like watering a plant; it's vital for growth.

3. Growth Opportunities: Picture an ambitious climber looking for the next ledge to hoist themselves up. Similarly, employees look for growth opportunities—be it learning, promotions, or new challenges. This drive to climb higher is a significant motivational force.

C. Power-Up: Tactics to Supercharge Workplace Motivation

1. Open Communication Channels: Whether it's a chat over coffee or a formal meeting, open dialogue ensures employees feel heard, valued, and connected.

2. Flexibility: Not all are night owls or early birds. Offering flexibility—be it in work hours or location—can significantly boost morale and motivation.

3. Team Building Activities: These aren't just fun breaks but vital tools to foster camaraderie, trust, and a shared sense of purpose.

4. Personal Development Plans: Tailored plans that cater to individual aspirations and strengths ensure employees see a clear path ahead, fueling their drive.

5. Feedback Loops: Constructive feedback isn't criticism; it's the compass that guides improvements. Regular feedback sessions ensure employees know their strengths and areas for growth.

Note to readers: The world of work isn't just cubicles and conference calls. It's a dynamic landscape of dreams, challenges, aspirations, and collaborations. At the heart of this landscape is motivation. Whether you're a leader or an intern, understanding and harnessing this force can transform professional journeys from mundane pathways into thrilling adventures.

Chapter 7: Dancing on the Edge: The Shadows of Motivation

Picture a brilliantly lit stage where dancers gracefully glide. But every spotlight casts a shadow. Motivation, while a force of positive propulsion, has its darker corners too. Let's venture into this less-trodden path to ensure we dance safely in the glow of motivation, avoiding the lurking shadows.

A. Too Much of a Good Thing? The Tricky Terrain of Over-Motivation

1. The Blurry Lines: There's a fine line between passionate persistence and unhealthy obsession. Sometimes, in the pursuit of our goals, we may push too hard, risking our well-being.

2. Burnouts and Exhaustion: Think of a car revving nonstop. It's bound to overheat! Similarly, constant high levels of motivation without breaks can lead to physical and mental burnouts.

3. Missing the Forest for the Trees: Over-motivation can sometimes make us narrowly focused, so much so that we may miss out on the bigger picture or ignore other vital aspects of life.

B. Golden Cages: The Subtle Snare of Extrinsic Motivation

1. Running After Carrots: Extrinsic motivation is when we're driven by external rewards, like bonuses or accolades. While they can be great boosters, relying solely on them is like a hamster running endlessly for a treat. It can be exhausting and unfulfilling.

2. The Fragility of External Rewards: What happens when the rewards stop, or change? Solely extrinsic motivation can be fragile. Today's bonus-driven employee might be tomorrow's disengaged worker if the bonus disappears.

3. Authenticity and Joy: While chasing after external motivations, we might lose touch with what genuinely brings us joy, leading to a life that's rich in rewards but poor in fulfillment.

C. Walking the Tightrope: Tips to Balance and Manage Motivation Levels

1. The Power of Pause: Regularly take a step back to assess your drive. Is it healthy? Is it aligned with your true self? Sometimes, a simple pause can provide profound insights.

2. Blend the Intrinsic and Extrinsic: Like a balanced diet, ensure your motivational sources are varied. Have some external goals, but also seek internal satisfaction.

3. Seek Feedback: Just as mirrors reflect our appearance, feedback from trusted individuals can reflect our motivational state. Are you pushing too hard? Are you being lured by mere rewards? Feedback helps you recalibrate.

4. Embrace Holistic Goals: Instead of narrowly focused

aims, have holistic goals that cater to varied facets of life—professional, personal, health, relationships, and more.

5. Celebrate Small Joys: Instead of just major milestones, learn to find joy in everyday moments. This ensures that motivation flows gently, like a stream, rather than in tumultuous torrents.

Note to readers: As with many things in life, balance is key. Motivation, while a potent force for good, has its potential pitfalls. Awareness is the first step to safety. As you dance in the radiant glow of motivation, may you be ever mindful of the shadows, treading with grace, wisdom, and joy.

Chapter 8: Navigating Tomorrow: Motivation's Exciting Horizon

Imagine standing on a cliff, watching the sunrise of a brand-new day. As its first rays kiss the horizon, there's a world of possibilities unfolding. That's the future of motivation—bright, evolving, and full of potential. Join us as we peer into the telescope of time to catch a glimpse of what's to come.

A. Charting New Waters: Predictions for Motivation Theory in the 21st Century

1. Beyond Borders: In an increasingly globalized world, motivation won't be restricted by geographies. What drives a teenager in Tokyo could be similar to a retiree in Toronto. Global trends will have localized impacts.

2. Digital Detox and Nature's Embrace: As people grapple with the pressures of the digital age, there will be a swing towards nature, mindfulness, and self-awareness as sources of motivation.

3. Personalization: With the rise of big data and analytics, products, services, and experiences will be tailored to individual motivational triggers. One-size-fits-all will be a relic of the past.

B. Silicon's Insight: AI and Machine Learning in Decoding Motivation

1. The Data Lens: Machines, with their vast data-processing capabilities, can spot patterns humans might overlook. This can offer fresh insights into what drives us, be it shopping habits or fitness routines.

2. Virtual Coaches: Imagine a digital companion that understands your motivational highs and lows, offering advice, support, or even a pep talk when needed. This isn't sci-fi—it's just around the corner.

3. Ethical Considerations: As AI delves into our motivational psyche, questions of privacy, data security, and ethical use of insights will take center stage. It's a thrilling, yet cautious road ahead.

C. The Motivational Mosaic: Fresh Concepts and Theories on the Horizon

1. Collective Motivation: As communities face global challenges, from climate change to pandemics, collective motivation —the drive of groups united by shared goals—will gain prominence.

2. Quantum Motivation: Borrowing from quantum physics, there's emerging talk of understanding motivation not just linearly but as a web of interconnected, often unpredictable, factors.

3. The Eudaimonic Drive: Moving beyond mere happiness or success, future motivation theories might delve deeper into 'eudaimonia'—the ancient Greek concept of a fulfilling, meaningful life.

Note to readers: As we stand on the cusp of tomorrow, gazing into the vast expanse of the future, it's heartening to see that the quest to understand what drives us—the essence of motivation—remains as vibrant as ever. Whether through the silicon circuits of AI or the age-old wisdom of philosophers, our journey of discovery continues. As you ride the waves of your own motivation, may you always be curious, open, and excited about the horizons yet to come.

Chapter 9: Crafting Your Drive: The Motivation Toolkit

Picture yourself in a cozy workshop, surrounded by an array of gleaming tools. Each is unique, with a specific purpose. That's what the realm of motivation is like—a well-stocked toolkit designed to help you carve, shape, and refine your drive. Let's roll up our sleeves and explore these tools together.

A. Mastering the Blueprint: Tools and Techniques for Assessing Motivation

1. Self-Reflection Journals: Think of this as a diary, but instead of recounting your day, you dive deep into your motives. What made you smile? What felt like a drag? Over time, patterns emerge, offering insights into your personal drivers.

2. Motivational Questionnaires: Simple sets of questions can often shine a light on areas of strength or aspects that need attention. No grades here; it's just a compass to guide your path.

3. Vision Boards: A collage of pictures, quotes, and aspirations. A visual representation of what you're striving towards can be a daily boost, reminding you of the 'why' behind your efforts.

B. The Inner Oasis: Mindfulness and Meditation in Boosting Motivation

1. The Breath's Magic: It sounds simple, but pausing to take a few deep breaths can declutter the mind, making room for clearer, more focused motivation.

2. Guided Meditations: Imagine a calm voice guiding you through a forest or along a beach, helping you connect with your inner desires and drives. That's the beauty of guided meditation—a journey inward.

3. The Art of Being Present: Mindfulness is about being in the moment. When we're fully present in what we do, the task itself becomes a source of joy, naturally amplifying our motivation.

C. Lessons from the Field: Hypothetical Case Studies of Winning Motivation Strategies

1. The Coffee Shop Dream: Lily always wanted to start a coffee shop. Instead of just dreaming, she broke it down into steps—learning about coffee, saving money, finding a location. Each step, fueled by clear motivation, led her to her dream café by the beach.

2. Climbing the Corporate Ladder: Raj wasn't driven by titles but by learning. In every role, he sought new skills, be it public speaking, project management, or mentoring. This thirst for growth propelled him to leadership roles, even without him aiming for them explicitly.

3. The Fitness Transformation: Sam struggled with consistency in workouts. Then, instead of vague goals like 'getting fit', he aimed for '20 push-ups non-stop' or 'running 3 miles'. These specific, tangible goals, coupled with a support group, transformed his motivation and physique.

Note to readers: Just as a skilled craftsperson knows which tool to use and when, understanding and leveraging your motivational tools can work wonders. It's a dynamic mix of introspection, techniques, and real-world inspirations. As you navigate your unique journey, may your toolkit be ever-handy, helping you mold, shape, and amplify your drive towards your dreams.

Chapter 10: To the Horizon and Beyond: Charting Our Motivated Futures

Imagine standing atop a hill after a long hike. The vista before you is breathtaking, and the sense of accomplishment, palpable. That's where we are now—at the culmination of our journey through the landscape of motivation. Let's take a moment to catch our breath, look back, and chart the course forward.

A. A Stroll Down Memory Lane: Recap of Key Points

1. Motivation's Essence: At its core, motivation is the 'why' behind our actions—the driving force pushing us to act, dream, and aspire.

2. History's Wisdom: From ancient philosophies to psychological pioneers, the quest to understand motivation has been a vibrant tapestry of insights and ideas.

3. Modern Times, Modern Drives: The digital age, with its swirl of technology, social media, and global interactions, has added new colors and contours to our motivational palette.

4. Tools at Hand: Recognizing our motivational triggers, harnessing techniques like mindfulness, and drawing from real-world success stories are our toolkit for a driven life.

B. Gazing into the Mirror: Personal Reflections on the Journey through Motivation Theory

1. The Universal and the Personal: While motivation theories offer broad insights, the true magic lies in their personal resonance. It's about finding the universal threads that weave into your unique tapestry.

2. The Dance of Light and Shadow: As with all things, motivation too has its sunlit spots and darker corners. Navigating it is a dance of balance, self-awareness, and growth.

3. The Endless Journey: Understanding motivation isn't a destination; it's a continuous journey. Each day offers new lessons, challenges, and joys in the realm of what drives us.

C. Passing the Torch: The Final Charge for a Motivated World

1. The Ripple Effect: One motivated individual can spark a chain reaction. Imagine a world where each of us, fueled by positive drive, sets off ripples of change, innovation, and growth.

2. Cultivating Communities: Building spaces—be they homes, workplaces, or online hubs—where motivation is nurtured, celebrated, and shared, paves the path for collective growth.

3. The Future Beckons: With the tools and insights at our disposal, and the vast expanse of the future ahead, it's up to us to craft a world where motivation flows freely, empowering dreams, aspirations, and actions.

Note to readers: As this chapter closes, it's not the end, but a new beginning. The pages of this book were but a guide. The true journey of motivation lies in your heart, your choices, and the mark you leave on the world. As you stride forth, may your steps be driven, your path clear, and your heart full of the vibrant energy of motivation.

About Freudian Trips

Welcome to Freudian Trips, your dedicated platform for diving deep into the world of psychology. We are more than just a YouTube channel or a book publisher. We are a beacon of enlightenment, making complex psychological concepts accessible and engaging for all.

Our YouTube channel is a rich repository of psychology made simple. We take the profound and often complex ideas from the world of psychology and break them down into digestible, easy-to-understand content. From the foundational theories of Freud to the cognitive insights of Piaget, we cover a broad spectrum of psychological schools and thoughts, making psychology accessible to everyone, regardless of their background or prior knowledge.

As a book publisher, we take the same approach, transforming intricate psychological theories into comprehensible narratives. Our books are not just collections of words, but vessels of wisdom that make psychology approachable and relatable. We believe that psychology should not be confined to academic circles, but should be available to all who seek to understand the human mind and behavior.

At Freudian Trips, we believe in the power of curiosity and the pursuit of knowledge. We are here to stoke the fires of your curiosity, to guide you on your intellectual journey, and to help you navigate the fascinating world of psychology.

If you are someone who is not afraid to question, to explore, and to learn, then you are in the right place. Join us on this journey of exploration, as we make psychology easy to understand, one concept at a time.

Be sure to visit our Youtube channel at: www.freudiantrips.com/youtube

You can also visit us on the web at www.freudiantrips.com

Welcome to The Freudian Trip community. Stay curious. Stay enlightened.

9 798863 150406